Lories and Lorikeets

A Complete Lorikeet Pet Guide

Lories Facts & Information, where to buy, health, diet, lifespan, mutations, breeding, fun facts and more!

By Lolly Brown

Copyrights and Trademarks

All rights reserved. No part of this book may be reproduced or transformed in any form or by any means, graphic, electronic, or mechanical, including photocopying, recording, taping, or by any information storage retrieval system, without the written permission of the author.

This publication is Copyright ©2017 NRB Publishing, an imprint. Nevada. All products, graphics, publications, software and services mentioned and recommended in this publication are protected by trademarks. In such instance, all trademarks & copyright belong to the respective owners. For information consult www.NRBpublishing.com

Disclaimer and Legal Notice

This product is not legal, medical, or accounting advice and should not be interpreted in that manner. You need to do your own due-diligence to determine if the content of this product is right for you. While every attempt has been made to verify the information shared in this publication, neither the author, neither publisher, nor the affiliates assume any responsibility for errors, omissions or contrary interpretation of the subject matter herein. Any perceived slights to any specific person(s) or organization(s) are purely unintentional.

We have no control over the nature, content and availability of the web sites listed in this book. The inclusion of any web site links does not necessarily imply a recommendation or endorse the views expressed within them. We take no responsibility for, and will not be liable for, the websites being temporarily unavailable or being removed from the internet.

The accuracy and completeness of information provided herein and opinions stated herein are not guaranteed or warranted to produce any particular results, and the advice and strategies, contained herein may not be suitable for every individual. Neither the author nor the publisher shall be liable for any loss incurred as a consequence of the use and application, directly or indirectly, of any information presented in this work. This publication is designed to provide information in regard to the subject matter covered.

Neither the author nor the publisher assume any responsibility for any errors or omissions, nor do they represent or warrant that the ideas, information, actions, plans, suggestions contained in this book is in all cases accurate. It is the reader's responsibility to find advice before putting anything written in this book into practice. The information in this book is not intended to serve as legal, medical, or accounting advice.

Foreword

Lories and lorikeets have been some of the most sought after parrot companions for a very long time. Its presence dates back some 2,500 years ago.

They may not rank as high up the popularity list of parrots, yet clamor for these birds have not let up since the revelations of their docile nature and natural curiosity. Notably recognized and admired for their remarkable vocal abilities and their uncanny talent for speech, these smallish exotic birds are natives of the dense forests of the regions of Australia, Polynesia, Papua New Guinea and parts of southeastern Asia. They are also prolific talkers who like to talk a lot and are often seen and heard as part of a squawking flock when foraging for food.

This book will provide many facts and information about the colorful breed of Lories and Lorikeets: its health, where to buy, its diet, how to breed them, its hybrids and more!

Table of Contents

Chapter One: Introduction 1

Chapter Two: What are Lories and Lorikeets? 5

    Facts about Lories and Lorikeets 7

        Quick Facts 11

    Other Fun Facts about Lories and Lorikeets 12

    Color Mutations of the Lories and Lorikeets 14

    Types of Lories 16

    Lories as Pets 19

    Lories and Lorikeets in History 20

Chapter Three: Lories and Lorikeets' Requirements 25

    Pros and Cons of Lories and Lorikeets 26

    Lories and Lorikeets Behavior with Other Pets 27

    Cost of Care 29

    Initial Costs 30

    Monthly Costs 30

Chapter Four: Tips in Buying Lories and Lorikeets 33

    Restrictions and Regulations in United States 35

    Permits in Great Britain and Australia 36

    Practical Tips in Buying Lories and Lorikeets 37

Chapter Five: Maintenance for Lories and Lorikeets 45

    Habitat and Environment 46

Ideal Cage Size for Lories and Lorikeets 48

Cage Maintenance 50

Diet and Feeding 57

Nutritional Needs of Lories and Lorikeets 59

Types of Food 60

Toxic Foods to Avoid 64

Handling and Training Lories and Lorikeets 65

Grooming Your Lories and Lorikeets 68

Basic Lories and Lorikeets Breeding Info 72

The Lories and Lorikeets Breeding Process 73

Hybridization of Lories and Lorikeets 77

Chapter Seven: Keeping Lories and Lorikeets Healthy 79

Common Health Problems 81

Recommended Tests 83

Signs of Possible Illnesses 85

Chapter Eight: Lories and Lorikeet in Summary 87

Basic Information 89

Cage Set-up Guide 90

Nutritional Information 91

Breeding Information 91

Glossary 103

Index 111

Photo Credits..117

References..119

Chapter One: Introduction

Lories and lorikeets have been some of the most sought after parrot companions for humans for a very long time. Its presence dates far back in history. It is has been said that Alexander the Great was one very proud keeper of some of these parrots species, which he saw and collected during his many travels across the seas The list henceforth just gets longer.

Chapter One: Introduction

Lories and lorikeets have also been consistently considered, and expected, to be regular aviary residents for over 2,500 years now. They may not rank as high up the popularity list of parrots yet clamor for these birds have not let up since the revelations of their docile nature and natural curiosity. Notably recognized and admired for their remarkable vocal abilities and their uncanny talent for speech, these smallish exotic birds are natives of the dense forests of the regions of Australia, Polynesia, Papua New Guinea and parts of southeastern Asia. They are colorfully garbed by nature in beautifully flamboyant plumage that will make anybody stop to admire these multi-hued forest dwellers.

This particular species of parrot is considered to be the most sociable of their sort, hence, the demand for these birds by avian enthusiasts and bird lovers. These birds, when exposed to human interaction, will not hesitate to satisfy its curiosity of you just as you are curious of it. Having a friendly nature, dexterity for acrobatic antics, and a penchant to entertain, it is no wonder the demand for them has not waned.

This feathered duo, whose name is distinguished by the length of its tail - Lories sport short tails whilst Lorikeets have a longer tail of plume - are equally adorable and

Chapter One: Introduction

surprisingly spry, quick, and playfully active. Each of these intelligent (hopefully) soon-to-be talkers is counted as a distinct class of species of and a close relation to other parrot kinds. There are over 55 species of Lories and Lorikeets in existence all over the world today.

They are said to have a lifespan of about 10-12 years in the wild. The length of life notably spikes up when the birds are raised in captivity, this is perhaps owed to the regular provision of food, better living conditions, medical attention, and the absence of larger animals out to prey on them,

Every novice pet keeper guardian needs a leg up and assistance to be able to raise their choice of pet properly. No pet owner would want to be the cause of illness of their pets because of misinformation or lack of knowledge. As you read on, you will find useful and informative chunks of information to help you become an effective keeper of Lories and Lorikeets. This is by no means an end to your search for further information and you are strongly encouraged to proactively research more on this breed of colorfully winged acrobats.

Allow us to reveal more about this well-balanced, easy to warm up to duo and get to know more about them,

Chapter One: Introduction

their health, how to house and care for them, their nutritional needs, how they are bred, their natural living conditions, their good and not so good traits and everything in between you will need to know to raise Lories and Lorikeets successfully.

Chapter Two: What are Lories and Lorikeets?

    These colorfully talkative birds have some are perhaps the most amiable and docile of all the parrot specie. This duo tends to warm up to people easily and is also quite the comic who likes to show off its acrobatic abilities. They are born entertainers who like to play, explore, and if given the proper training, are chatty companions who can be taught to do simple tricks. They are flock oriented avian and get on quite famously with other birds with which they can chat with and those equally sized as they.

Chapter Two: What are Lories and Lorikeets?

They are a bunch of very social birds that hop from tree to tree in search of their favorite meals - nectar and pollen. These prolific talkers and like to talk a lot and are often seen and heard as part of a squawking flock when foraging for food. Always on alert for predators who would like to make them their next meal, lories and lorikeets call out warning signals to warn other birds of the flock of a predator in their midst.

Once satiated and full they make their way back to their homes and are generally quite after feeding, only making noise when a predator is sensed or spotted. When a predator is near an alarm call is made to give warning to others. Predators are kept at bay because of the danger-signal system these birds give off.

There are a number of things that need to be kept in mind by any individual wanting to take in Lories and Lorikeets and you will find more useful information to these birds in the next following chapters.

Chapter Two: What are Lories and Lorikeets?

Facts about Lories and Lorikeets

There are around 55 various species of these colorfully, chatty birds and this is just in the *Loriinae* group of parrots! A mere 12 of these smallish, colorful, and intelligent, comics and talkers are taken in as family pets. Amongst the large family of parrots and their many sorts, Lori and Lorikeets are most sought after as pets. This is mainly because of their easy-going manner, their ability to warm up to people easily and their penchant for entertaining.

Lories and Lorikeets are quite different from other parrot species because of the specialized diet they need. Unlike the other parrot species, Lories and Lorikeets do not feed off seeds. Instead they have evolved to live on pollen and nectar and in fact cannot manage to feed on seeds like their other parrot cousins.

They possess a tongue with a unique quality which allows them to feed on these kinds of sustenance. Alternately called honey eaters, this colorful duo both have unique paint brush like tongues which they use get nectar and pollen, a staple of their diet which they harvest from flowers.

Chapter Two: What are Lories and Lorikeets?

Lories and Lorikeets are deft acrobats, innately playful, and naturally curious creatures. Keepers of these sorts find the everyday activities of the birds to be captivatingly amusing and entertaining. With a little bit of time and patience, you'll discover that Lories and Lorikeets will impress you by showing off their speaking skills, learning to talk as they mimic people around them with many possessing good vocabularies that only tend to improve with time.

In the wild, Lories and lorikeets live in large flocks. Contingent of the species, Lories and Lorikeets are by nature from the Southeast Asian archipelago and regions around Australia. In search of food, these birds will fly from island to island. The perambulate rainbow lorikeet will go to where eucalyptus flowers bloom all along the coast of Australia.

Lories and Lorikeets are able to thrive for about 7 to 10 years when out in the wild. In captivity, zoo captivity particularly, these small chatterboxes enjoy a longer lifespan compared to their cousins in the wild, and live for as long as 15 years.

It is safe to assume that the birds, living in a controlled environment, enjoy better health are free of stress they would otherwise experience if in the wild, are given

Chapter Two: What are Lories and Lorikeets?

medical attention, as well as regular meals of a proper and balanced diet - not to mention, a whole lot of activities that allow them to interact with and be around humans and their sort.

A healthy body is usually followed by a sharp mind. Being given all the space and exercise these actively playful flyers require, as well as frequent socialization to stimulate the mind, Lories and lorikeets in captivity can be said to live sheltered lives. Many may argue that Lories and lorikeets in captivity are deprived of living free lives in the wild. And they could have a point.

But it is also owed to zoos that those in their care is given a chance to live free from predators and from humans who may hunt them for game, money, or because they are considered agricultural pests. It's an argument that has a fine line.

Given the privilege of witnessing this playful duo, and their other kin, in a habitat meant to mimic their natural environment, we can learn more about these special sorts of parrots whilst admiring their silky-looking, shiny and colorful appearance and get to hear them show off their dexterity for speech in person as we are entertained by their comical antics.

Chapter Two: What are Lories and Lorikeets?

Lories and lorikeets have an average length of 6-15 inches, depending on the species, and they have a general weight of about 20 to 280 grams, also depending on the species as some Lories and lorikeets a tad larger or smaller than others.

Telling Lories and lorikeets from the other parrot sorts is almost impossible to do just by looking at them. It is their unique tongue which looks like a fork or a brush that would be a good giveaway of their identities. To tell a Lory from a lorikeet is a tad simpler, because their tails are what give them away - with Lories sporting short, blunt tail feathers and lorikeets displaying a longer and pointed tail.

Most of the birds in this family of parrots are frequent flyers that commute in flocks and hop from island to island for the purposes of foraging for food.

These amazingly intelligent birds are pretty adaptable to most climates and can withstand both cold and hot temperatures within considerable limits, which works for them because in their natural environment, the mountain ranges they reside at can become pretty chilly come night time.

Chapter Two: What are Lories and Lorikeets?

Quick Facts

Have jealousy issues? Put your ego away and brace your sensitive heart for the extremely social Lories and Lorikeets. As grateful as they will be of your care and love, don't take it personally if they seem to warm up easily to total strangers. This curious duo not only likes the attention humans give them, they eagerly reciprocate the attention and are just as curious as their handlers and admirers.

Given time, they will understand you to be the primary player responsible for their life on Easy Street. Lories and Lorikeets have thrived and survived on flowers, pollen, fruits, nectar and the occasional hapless treat, a succulent insect. Exercise your green thumb and sow seeds and grow a pot of hibiscus. This flowery plant is an excellent source of food and vitamins for the busy Lories.

These bird sorts are athletic players and will leave you out of breath by simply watching them hop, roll, fly, perch, wrestle, and hang around their digs. They are also extremely intelligent and trainable. Exercise your patience and get them a good trainer and you'll soon be amazed at the dexterity of their mimicking abilities.

Chapter Two: What are Lories and Lorikeets?

They spend a portion of their time grooming each other, helping the other to clean hard to reach places. Much like other parrots, Lories and Lorikeets typically have one partner and can breed throughout the year. However, Lories and Lorikeets from southern Australia only breed between the months of August and January.

In the wild they nest high above ground level usually in the hollows of trees. The nests they build are usually harvested from decayed wood. Both male and female roost together but it would only be the female who would sit (or incubate) their two small, white eggs.

Males do help once the baby birds are reborn by feeding them. Lories' and Lorikeets' chicks once hatched appear with closed eyes and no feathers at all. The chicks, as they grow, will gradually grow the unmistakable, colorful plumage they inherited from their parents. It will be about seven to eight weeks before the babies learn to fly.

Other Fun Facts about Lories and Lorikeets

A German zoologist and naturalist, Heinrich Kuhl, well-known for publishing monographs and petrels and for

Chapter Two: What are Lories and Lorikeets?

observing and reporting on the creatures of Java is whose name Kuhl's lorikeet is named after.

The nomadic lorikeet is just crazy over flowering eucalyptus and will fly and hop to areas where these plants bloom at the proper time of the year.

Appearing in the popular first edition of The Parrots of the World is the marvelously Rainbow Lorikeet. This is the same species of parrot which also appeared in the Books of Australia lithographs by John Gould.

Some of the more persistent predators who prey upon Lories and lorikeets are larger sized birds like peregrine falcons, whistling kites and brown falcons. On terra, Lories and lorikeets in the sights and reach of pythons will likelier than not be dinner to these reptiles.

Lories are set apart from the other parrot sort for the reason that they eat pollen and nectar instead of seed like their other winged cousins. Due to their finicky, specialized diets, first-time bird keepers/guardians are discouraged from taking them in as pets. The sensitivity of their diet calls for an experienced and present guardian/keeper who is aware of its special needs and provides these to them to maintain overall good bird-health.

Chapter Two: What are Lories and Lorikeets?

Color Mutations of the Lories and Lorikeets

The various species of Lories and lorikeets are stunningly beautiful birds sporting shiny and very colorful plumage. The lorikeet is smaller and can be identified by its long pointed tail. Its body color is usually green with patches of yellow and red. On the other hand, Lories are heavier-bodied, larger than lorikeets and have shorter tails which are blunt. Lories usually have a red body with patches of purple, green and yellow.

Mutations and hybrids of Lories appear generally have one or two features that differ from the normal one. Common feature variations can be seen in the plumage color and may also include a difference in the beak. There are some instances where weight and body size can differ, depending on how it was bred.

Tropical Lories and lorikeets are larger than other lories/lorikeet species. They are known to be better talkers than their smaller Australian cousins. They are also known for their deft ability to mimic what they hear often. This bunch of birds are extremely energetic, boisterous, smart and are quite loud therefore not the recommended sort for people who live in close proximity to their neighbors.

Chapter Two: What are Lories and Lorikeets?

Keeper guardians of the tropical Lories and lorikeet should be committed and patient as they can cause quite a ruckus with their squawking.

Australian Lories and lorikeets are the smaller of the *Loriinae* species and are known to be relatively quiet. They are apartment-dweller favorites because of the minimal sounds they make. They are equally charming and sweet and make lovable family pets.

Naturally occurring genetic variations are mutations with interests toward the colored mutations displaying a difference in the color of its plumage. The reasons why a lot of aviculturists work on producing mutations is to produce striking plumage colors that are uncommonly found in nature, the rarity of color variation and of course, these unique mutations fetch a much higher price in the market compared to the "normal" colored sort.

There are breeders who have produced a new line of mutations in some Lory species. They do this by hybridizing a color mutation of one type of Lory to a different one. Most breeders frown upon this production of unnatural mutation and hybrid and deem this practice unacceptable. Other perceives this as creating new variations.

Chapter Two: What are Lories and Lorikeets?

Mutations in nature constantly occur amongst Lories, however, color mutations are not. With the exception of the grey/green color mutation of the Scaly lorikeet, color mutations in nature are not common at all. This is perhaps due to the large gene pool wild Lories. Naturally occurring mutations are eventually bred out rapidly. Another reason for naturally occurring color mutations not likely to populate successfully is their susceptibility of predators preying on them.

Lories and lorikeets in captivity would have a higher chance of establishing color mutations because the available gene-pool would be much smaller and inbreeding would be more likely. Breeding for the purpose of color mutation is not as simple as it would seem, given the circumstances mentioned, because this process does not ensure the reliability of producing color mutations and will likely take many years and many birds to establish a new sort.

Types of Lories

There are at least a dozen species of lories and lorikeets that are favored by avian enthusiasts, bird aficionados and pet bird keepers everywhere. Some of the species provided here are the most popular as pets:

Chapter Two: What are Lories and Lorikeets?

Green-Naped Lorikeet

The *Trichoglossus haematodus haematodus*, otherwise known as the green-naped lorikeet, is perhaps the most common subspecies of the rainbow lorikeet taken in as pets and raised in captivity. In addition, it is also one of the most brightly colored parrots.

It has a rich blue head with a patch of lemon-yellow at the back and its beak. Its head is rich blue with a lemon-yellow patch at the back and an orange colored red beak.

Both its back and wings display a splash of bright-green color, and its puffed breast is streaked with a deep, dark blue and magenta.

The green-naped lorikeet is about 10 inches long in length and has a tendency to be an engaging talker, often heard deftly mimicking noises around it that it hears.
There are presently other subspecies of rainbow lorikeet which are available in the hobby.

Chattering Lory

The *Lorius garrulus* species, better known as the chattering lory, has a predominantly bright red color with green legs and wings. The chattering Lory is about 12 inches (30.5 cm) in length, measuring from beak to tail. This bird is an adept talker and a fast mimic. In the wild, chattering Lories have been deemed and listed endangered. However, in captivity, there are a good number of them bred as pets.

Red Lory

The *Eos bornea*, also known as the red Lory, is a name befitting this surprisingly vibrant lory bird. Its bright red plumage is accentuated electric blue markings on its wings. The red Lory is about 12 inches (30.5 cm) in length. The *eos bornea* is one of the meeker parrots, not much for a chatter, and preferring mimic noises around it it hears instead.

Black Capped Lory

The Black Capped Lory is a medium sized lory and is a stocky looking bird with a short, slightly stubby tail. This Lory is the second largest of all the Lories subfamily. These brightly colored birds commonly develop very strong bonds with their keeper guardians. This consistency in its bonding tendency is characteristic of their habits in the wild of bonding only to one or two other birds.

Chapter Two: What are Lories and Lorikeets?

The playful and animating, Black Capped Lory, makes for an excellent pet and suitable company to those willing and committed to providing it significant and meaningful attention.

Ongoing obedience training is strongly recommended for this Lory species, as the black capped Lory can be quite an earful. Continuous training to prevent this from becoming an issue is advised.

They have the potential to be excellent talkers and are very warm and affectionate. They enjoy a long life span with an average range of 20-25 years.

Lories as Pets

A serious keeper guardian will need to invest in a large enclosure that would house their new bird pet in because they are quite active and will require lots of leg and wing room to move around.

These parrot sorts, the Lories and lorikeets are amiable birds who easily warm up to people and make friends. They tame easily, are easily trained with a measure of patience and are excellent pet companions.

Chapter Two: What are Lories and Lorikeets?

You will do lot of work daily in order for the lorikeets' enclosure to maintain cleanliness as the lorikeet is a random pooper and can make quite a mess when it let's go and bombs away!

These playfully active, energetic species of Lories will need lots and lots of curiosities to check out and play with inside of their enclosure, to ensure a good measure of physical activity and to routinely stimulate its mind to help keep its wits sharp.

A Lory can make a wonderful pet for the right household. Owners enjoy his clownish antics and vivacious personality. However, he is a highly energetic bird who needs a lot of attention, as well as a specialized diet. Properly preparing for your Lory will help both of you live many happy years together.

Lories and Lorikeets in History

These brilliantly colorful and extremely intelligent birds, Lories and lorikeets, are strictly arboreal and can be usually found in mangroves, forests and eucalyptus groves foraging for their favorite and staple diet of flowers, nectar and pollen.

Chapter Two: What are Lories and Lorikeets?

They originate from the tropical countries nearby and around the Australian region like New Zealand, Papua New Guinea. Some of them are found in the Philippines and others are natives of Indonesia. They flock by the multitude and sometimes in the thousands, typically flying in a large group, blanketing the sky as they fly along. They frequent places they have been to and they know, historically, to be abundant with food they need for sustenance.

It is their colorfully bright hues and smaller size that help Lories and lorikeets conceal themselves amongst plantation and tree foliage. This is nature's way of helping them keep safe and away from potential predators like snakes and birds of prey out to make a Lory or a lorikeet its next meal. They are an arboreal species and choose to nest high above the ground, inside the hollow spaces of trees.

Flying, foraging for food, and socializing in large numbers give them the advantage of having many eyes, ears and senses alert, against potential predators, for each of their own safety, as well as the other birds of the flock. "Safety in numbers" is a natural rule amongst Lories and lorikeets and has gotten them this far.

Chapter Two: What are Lories and Lorikeets?

These small, island trippers prefer to fly and stay together closely in large flocks helping them stay safe with most, if not all, of them mindfully alert of their surroundings. The more their eyes stake out their chosen territory when foraging for food means a higher likelihood of safety and/ or escape.

These parrot species possess a uniquely brush like tongue which help them dine on the only sort of foods their beaks and tongue allow. They fly from place to place in search of nectar, pollen and flowers and on occasion will enjoy a meaty insect along the way. The beak of the Lory and lorikeet is the perfect utilitarian tool, provided by nature and natural occurrence, designed especially for the eating convenience of this parrot sort that cannot eat seeds.

The beak of both Lories and lorikeet are both equally capable of crushing flowers. Their fork-like tongue, a unique feature setting them apart from other parrot species, is used to sop up the nectar they draw expertly out of the flower. Unlike their other parrot cousins, Lories and lorikeets possess weak gizzards and crop because of their specialized diet.

Lories and lorikeets are skilled creatures designed by nature to gather and collect particles of pollen which they deftly pack into little bundles of pellets which makes for

Chapter Two: What are Lories and Lorikeets?

easier dining. Their acrobatic dexterity in nature is employed to get to all the flowers on the trees of the mangroves and forests they visit, whilst they hang upside down from branches.

These highly social birds travel in large and loud flocks, to avoid the dangers of predators, go from one tree to the next in search of nectar from flowers. They are quite a loud bunch when eating as they excitedly chatter throughout their meal. After leaving the grounds where they feed them all retrace their flight and head back home. Whilst resting in their snug nests typically fashioned from damp dead wood, these birds are typically quiet. These pretty loud, and vocal avian would only make a noisy fuss to give others of the flock warning of the presence of a predator.

Many of them like to while time away by grooming and helping a partner reach and clean spots that are hard to reach. This specie of parrot, like most other parrot species, typically chooses one partner and stay with them. There is no specific breeding period for Lories and lorikeets that usually breed any time of the year. Save for the Australian Lories and lorikeets that usually breed from September to March each year, other Lories and lorikeets can sometimes produce eggs twice a year.

Chapter Two: What are Lories and Lorikeets?

Lories and lorikeets choose to nest in the hollow of trees high above the ground using decayed wood for bedding in their nests. Both Lory and lorikeet partners would typically roost together during a breeding spell and each take up specific tasks for their little brood. It is the female bird's job to sit on and incubate the eggs she laid whilst the male bird will take the responsibility of foraging for and feeding its offspring. The eggs, once hatched, reveal two very tiny, fragile featherless hatchlings with eyes shut like slits.

Not all *Loriinae* species are endangered; however, they all have one big problem - the threat of humans. These little, colorful avian are hunted and killed for their colorful feathers and are captured to be sold as pets to many countries, notwithstanding bird-protection laws currently in effect.

Another reason for disappearing bird species is the continued practice of illegal logging, compromising trees which provide them shelter and sustenance. In Australia some of the *Loriinae* species are considered pests to agriculture and farming. Concerned land owners and their employees can be given permission to destroy them on sight given they have obtained a license to do so and under special conditions.

Chapter Three: Lories and Lorikeets' Requirements

A budding Lory and Lorikeet keeper - one who is determined and committed to being guardian to these marvelously unique winged beings - should factor in the additional responsibility of caring for the colorfully winged avian for the long haul.

It will require occasional medical attention, supplies and sundries for its daily upkeep, food provisions on a daily basis, ample attention and interaction with keeper,

Chapter Three: Lories and Lorikeets' Requirements

supervised out-of-cage forays, a safe environment where a Lory and/or a Lorikeet can confidently cohabitate with a partner sans fear or trepidation.

Lories and lorikeets require a lot of attention and can fall into depression if not paid any mind by their keeper guardians. They can be quite aggressive if their space and possessions are not respected.

Pros and Cons of Lories and Lorikeets

Their specialized diet is the only real drawback and reason for potential human keepers to question their capabilities and means as to whether they are in fact ready to take on the task of rearing this colored avifauna pair.

If a responsible adult keeper is committed and able to give the Lory and Lorikeet the proper and adequate care they need and make available provisions for their especially unique dietary needs, then the Lory might be the perfect bird for you to raise and care for.

Another question a potential keeper of Lories and Lorikeets need to ask themselves is "Is there enough space in my home to house these small to medium sized birds in a cage large enough (if not ridiculously big for a pair of tiny flyers) for the wee creatures to reside comfortably? As

Chapter Three: Lories and Lorikeets' Requirements

mentioned earlier, the short-tailed Lory and the long-tailed Lorikeet are an active and playful duo needing space to romp and room for light rough housing. Answer that truthfully and you would've come closer to making a decision on getting one, a pair or more.

Trouble may and will likely arise should two Lories and/or lorikeets share space and furnishings. These species are quite protective of their possessions and may attack and injure the other bird introduced to its enclosure. To avoid a messy battle from ensuing, make sure that the pair that will be sharing enclosure is a paired couple.

Lories and Lorikeets Behavior with Other Pets

The thought of placing a varied species of birds in the same aviary or enclosure is probably as ancient as keeping birds in captivity as pets.

Placing a variety of bird species is quite complex and sadly there are no set guidelines or methods that are foolproof with the idea of combining an assortment of species since all birds have their individuality and each have their own intricacies and unpredictability.

Chapter Three: Lories and Lorikeets' Requirements

The birds which are usually peaceful and placid may develop to become aggressive in a variety of situations whilst others that are known for their aggressive behavior may usually be placed in with an assorted collective and they will be able to thrive and live in peace together.

The challenge of placing a mix of a variety of bird species is inversely proportional to the size of the aviary or enclosure they are provided. Rule of thumb is; the larger the cage, the fewer challenges for the birds and ultimately fewer problems for the keeper guardian in caring for each, providing for all and individual training.

House similar sized parrot species together. Housing smaller parrot's species with larger ones could pose their own problems of aggression. The bigger bird may fight for space, wake up on the wrong side of the perch and attack the smaller birds as an unfavorable reaction.

Unless Lories and lorikeets are bonded as a pair, housing two in one enclosure can pose a problem with one attacking the other. Keep this in mind if in consideration of housing two Lories and/or lorikeets in one enclosure.

Chapter Three: Lories and Lorikeets' Requirements

Cost of Care

Lories and lorikeets are surprisingly energetic avian. These parrot species are active birds in the wild and in captivity. If you want them to thrive they will have to be housed in furnished cages that are fitted with an assortment of sundries that would be appropriate to help spend their energy.

Not providing them with enough social interaction play and exercise, may lead to undesirable or worse, detrimental behaviors, like feather plucking - which is a disturbing sight to see. Since there are a variety of species of Lory and lorikeet, it is important to do fairly exhaustive research on the particular species you are in search of to determine its specific care requirement. It is impossible to give Lory and lorikeet care guidelines that will be true for all species.

Do not forget their specialized diet which sets them apart from other parrot species. The need for their diet has compelled bird food manufacturers to come up with products suitable for their diet and eating habits.

Chapter Three: Lories and Lorikeets' Requirements

Initial Costs

Be sure that you deal with breeds of the species and not any random internet offer promising to deliver a healthy Lory and/or lorikeet. Thankfully, this specie of parrot is not on any endangered list but you still wouldn't want to label an irresponsible keeper for dealing with sellers who may have acquired their birds from the wild.

Lories and Lorikeets will vary in price depending on the country, breeder and dealer. The price range for any of this duo is anywhere from $300-$900.

Factor in the expense of their enclosure which should be large enough to allow them to fly, as well as furnishings the enclosure must be fitted with for them to be able to hone and sharpen all their many talents for which they are well known.

Monthly Costs

Monthly costs of Lories and lorikeets will include expenses for their daily nutrition, and not much more after the initial investment on its enclosure and the enclosures fittings and furnishings.

Chapter Three: Lories and Lorikeets' Requirements

Every month your Lories and Lorikeets needs a varied and healthy diet. There's a massive selection of high quality seed diets, complete food and pelleted foods to choose from both online and in your local pet stores, not to mention some treats you might want to buy especially when they're doing tricks. The cost will depend on the brand as well as the nutritional value of the food. Feeding a variety of these foods, alongside fruits and vegetables is the key to a healthy parrot.

As for their grooming part or cage maintenance, you don't need brand new cleaning supplies every month, but of course, you will run out of bird shampoo and soap eventually. Just include it in your budget.

When it comes to medical care, unlike other birds, Lories rarely get sick but it's important to keep them healthy by taking them to an avian vet for medical check-up every now and then. Avian vets are trained specifically to work with exotic birds whereas a general practicing vet may not be familiar with their needs and treatments especially if they are sick, not to mention the medicines needed. If in case, this happens it's better and wiser to set aside a portion of your budget for any medical needs that will come up.

Chapter Three: Lories and Lorikeets' Requirements

In addition to all of these monthly costs you should plan for occasional extra costs like repairs to your bird's cage, replacement toys, food supplements, medicines and accessories. You won't have to cover these costs every month but you should include it in your budget to be safe.

Chapter Four: Tips in Buying Lories and Lorikeets

Here are facts important to know and worth researching on more for the serious keeper bent on sharing space with these feathered dynamic duo. 2,500 years of recorded existence and popularity has put many of these colorfully feathered pet-favorite. Sadly many of their kin and parrot cousins have been recognized to have dwindled in numbers recently.

Chapter Four: Tips in Buying Lories and Lorikeets

Recent years has been witness to more and more parrot sanctuaries and parrot rescues cropping up which indicate a rise in misinformed and uninformed once-keeper of these birds.

Before deciding to acquire a Lory or a lorikeet, it is vital for the potential keeper guardian to research and become better familiar with national and international trade regulations in relation to parrots. With more and more parrot species endangered in the wild, even parrot species not on the endangered list are now protected by the Convention on International Trade in Endangered Species of Wild Fauna and Flora (CITES).

Purchasing parrots is by no means illegal but the potential keeper guardian will have to follow a set of rules and certain regulations made to avoid and stave off the proliferation of endangered parrots illegally caught in the wild from entering the market.

Keep in mind that the national laws in your country can be different from international regulations therefore it is your responsibility to familiarize yourself with these laws. The following information aims to disclose what is lawfully allowed and what is illegal. As the potential keeper guardian of a Lory and/or lorikeet it will be up to you, the future keeper of these birds, to determine details of regulations for your own home country.

Restrictions and Regulations in United States

In the United States, importation of any of the species belonging to the parrot family is restricted. This is to prevent introduction of communicable diseases that can be passed on from parrots to humans. To be allowed and be given permission to import any parrot species for commercial purposes, whether to exhibit in aviary parks or zoos, and for purposes of scientific studies, permission to do so must be obtained from the Surgeon General of the United States Public Health Services. Permission is to be obtained by any concerned party requesting to import the parrots.

A formal application must be filled out and the approval of the Surgeon General must be given before the parrots are transmitted to the United States. When in the country, the birds will be quarantined and tested for a variety of diseases of which they may be carriers of and that could potentially be transmitted and pose danger to the local population.

There are three classifications for birds of the parrot family seeking approval for entry. The first is a privately

Chapter Four: Tips in Buying Lories and Lorikeets

owned shipment which is not to be more than three parrot species, accompanied by the person who owns the birds. The owner will have to show proof that the birds have been pets for about two years and no less. The person carrying the parrots in will also have to prove that the birds are not intended to be bartered, sold, exhibited or given away.

Shipments meant for zoo display or scientific study can contain any number of birds and must be recognized by the institutions, like zoos and bird parks which operate under public authority.

Commercial shipments are any number of parrots seeking entry to the US not specifically covered by the two previous classifications. Conditions of entry include the consideration of the parrot's age. Parrots may be permitted to enter if they are greater than 8-months old.

Permits in Great Britain and Australia

Pet owners and bird breeders are presently allowed to keep lorikeets and Lories without a license after regulations of ownership of such parrot species were revised. There are a total of 41 native bird species which can be traded or kept without the need of a license. On the other hand, license to destroy species which cause damage agriculture or private

Chapter Four: Tips in Buying Lories and Lorikeets

properties are given by the concerned wildlife state authorities. Licenses to destroy destructive bird species are only granted only if the species populations in question are in large numbers.

A grave offense of capturing these birds from the wild for captive breeding purposes is illegal and an offender caught is given a penalty to the tune of $4000. A total ban on trade overseas for native Australian birds came into effect in December of 1959 and attempts to relax these existing laws have all been thwarted and rejected.

Practical Tips in Buying Lories and Lorikeets

As a future companion and keeper of Lories and lorikeets you will want to make sure that you and the birds you purchase are positioned at an advantage. Before you close any deals you will want to ask questions and get upfront answers. Getting an ill bird can pose a bigger problem that can be harmful to humans.

You will want to determine the origin of the birds. You should never try to purchase a bird from overseas because it is primarily illegal and any bird getting into a market could potentially be a carrier of diseases that could cause outbreaks. It is not recommended for households with

Chapter Four: Tips in Buying Lories and Lorikeets

young children and pregnant mothers to own Lories and lorikeets as pets.

You will want to have an avian vet on your speed dial before you acquire the birds. You must take time to set an appointment with a list of prepared questions relevant to the care and husbandry of the birds you intend to bring home. Since Lories and lorikeets are not anywhere near the endangered list of birds, there is absolutely no reason to purchase a Lory or a lorikeet captured from the wild. You want to do your bit and check out local breeders of these birds, bird shelters, and bird sanctuaries.

You'd be surprised as to how little research is done by a few individuals who would later realize they took on more than they can handle and gave up the birds to aviaries, shelters and bird sanctuaries.

Observe the bird in its habitat and check for anomalies that belie a healthy bird. A healthy bird should be sprite, active, perky, lively, mobile, can stand on two feet, and both eyes and ears clear and alert.

Observe its appetite and drinking habits. Does it eagerly eat its food and drink water? Study its feathers and look for the presence of balding or bald spots. Its feathers

Chapter Four: Tips in Buying Lories and Lorikeets

should lay close to the body, not out of place, ruffled or continuously fluffed.

Both feet and legs of the bird must be free of bumps or lumps, should be smooth and there should be no signs of rough scales or scabs. The bird must show a keenness to communicate once socialized. It is not uncommon for these birds to be shy when in a new environment surrounded by new people and should soon warm up to the visiting company.

Confident and curious birds are signs of it being in good health. They can also show caution and awareness of surroundings and strangers too. It is recommended that you have your bird seen by an avian vet on a yearly basis to undergo health exams.

How to Find a Lories and Lorikeets Breeders

There are a number of ways to locate a Lory and a lorikeet breeder. You can ask individual you know are keepers of Lories and lorikeets for possible contacts. You may ask your local bird shelter or bird sanctuary if they can point you to the direction of a reputable bird breeder.

Chapter Four: Tips in Buying Lories and Lorikeets

You can seek a breeder online but will have to consider the breeders validity and reputation. You will want to see the bird for yourself, if logistically possible. You will need to witness the behavior and characteristics of the bird whilst under the care of the breeder.

You will only want to purchase birds with proper leg band identification which is to be provided by the breeder. Information such as date of birth, clutch number and the breeder number should be indicated. The bands serve as proof that the birds were bred locally and not undocumented or smuggled into the country.

List of Websites for Lories and Lorikeets Breeders in United States:

Bird Farm
http://www.birdfarm.com/sale/lories.asp

Birds Now
http://www.birdsnow.com/lory.htm

Bird Breeders
http://www.birdbreeders.com/birds/category/lories-and-lorikeets

Chapter Four: Tips in Buying Lories and Lorikeets

Exclusively Lories
http://www.exclusivelylories.com/

Chloe Sanctuary
http://chloesanctuary.org/

Lory Website
http://www.lorywebsite.com/

List of Websites for Lories and Lorikeets Breeders in United Kingdom:

Birds 4 Sale
http://www.birds4sale.co.uk/birds/269

UK Lories
http://uklories.co.uk/

Bird Trader UK
http://www.birdtrader.co.uk/parrots-for-sale/lories-for-sale

Buyilo UK
http://www.buyilo.co.uk/bird-breeders?i=oz-1114-5250395~5337593690

Chapter Four: Tips in Buying Lories and Lorikeets

Selecting a Healthy Lories and Lorikeets

Selecting a healthy Lory and a healthy lorikeet is vital to your success in raising healthy birds with no medical conditions or illnesses. It is imperative that you get to know how to spot weaknesses, abnormalities and anomalies in the bird before closing any deals to purchase. You want to avoid buying a bird you have not seen, so it is best to look for Lory and lorikeet breeders in your general area to have the advantage of visiting it in its present abode and see for yourself the condition and disposition of the bird of which you inquire.

Healthy Lories and lorikeets are actively, lively, playful and alert. They are sharp, intelligent and mobile. Healthy birds are able to support itself on both feet steadfastly and their feet and legs should be smooth with no signs of lumps, bumps, scars or rough scales.

Their feather is to be smoothed down on its body and not continuously fluffed not should there be bald spots or falling feathers. Their eyes and ears should be free of any liquid discharge and their beaks should not have deformities or be chipped.

Chapter Four: Tips in Buying Lories and Lorikeets

Healthy birds vocalize by clicking, chirping, whistling and mimicking words they picked up from handlers. They should show interest for conversation and must show keenness to communicate.

The bird is curious and displays confidence but should also display awareness of surroundings and new people and show a measure of caution to new and strange environments and situations.

Chapter Four: Tips in Buying Lories and Lorikeets

Chapter Five: Maintenance for Lories and Lorikeets

St. George Mivart, in his 1896 book, describes the playfully active and dressed to the nines Lorie to be "a quarrelsome and noisy bird" what with the constant cacophony of exchanged chatter between and amongst themselves. On the other hand, it's been observed that captive Lories that are hand fed by their keepers can be genuinely loving, entertaining pets ready to eagerly engage and amuse you to your heart's delight.

Chapter Five: Maintenance for Lories and Lorikeets

Prepare ahead for the arrival of your Lory and lorikeet pairs by getting all the necessary equipment you would need to house and care for the birds. Sort out your budget and get a list of what you will need to purchase and look for suppliers that carry those items. Once you have purchased its enclosure be sure to outfit and furnish the enclosure with all the necessary playthings to help in its much needed physical activity and to recreate a habitat not quite close but basically similar to its natural habitat.

Let's discuss the basic needs and requirements of Lories and lorikeets to find out how a potential keeper of these beautiful creations of nature can effectively raise them successfully. After all, with the lengthy lifespan observed of Lories and lorikeets, it is but wise to buckle down comfortably and look forward to a long relationship of co-dependency.

Habitat and Environment

The enclosures of the Lory and the lorikeet will be their own little slice of heaven. These typically territorial birds are sociable but prefer a space they can call their own. Lories and lorikeets are quite possessive of their property so if you are in the market to get more than one of these marvelously feathered birds; make sure that each one has

Chapter Five: Maintenance for Lories and Lorikeets

their own space, that they each are given enclosure equipment and toys exclusively for them.

The preparation of the birds' enclosure must have been completed - or semi completed - before the arrival of its new occupants. You may later add on other furnishings to the cage if you haven't already fitted it with necessary equipment. Be sure that the enclosure is large enough for the bird to flutter about without clipping its wings.

Something important to remember for a keeper guardian when bringing home their baby Lory and lorikeet is to minimize stress to the birds. Too much handling during this period may cause more harm than good. You will want to give the baby bird a chance to get used to its new enclosure and environment. Allow it about 3-4 days to get used to each fitting, furnishing and area of their enclosure.

Making sure that your Lory and lorikeet get the proper furnishings in their enclosures makes for a warm welcome and assures the birds of a special area which is a territory all their own. Once familiarized with its surroundings it will then start looking for company and companionship at which time you can step into the picture.

Chapter Five: Maintenance for Lories and Lorikeets

During the period of it getting familiar with its new home, make your presence felt by calling out soft sounds whilst in its ear shot and hearing range.

This is a non-invasive way of saying hello and the bird should get used to you sooner rather than later.

Ideal Cage Size for Lories and Lorikeets

Lories and lorikeets need their space to be able to spread their wings inside their abode. Aside from periodic, supervised forays outside its enclosure, it will naturally attempt to take flight and go from perch to perch. You will want to choose a cage that is the largest possible one as this doesn't only make your Lories and lorikeets happier but will give your pet Lory and lorikeet bird's better results when in training.

Keeping these birds in small cages will result in more challenges for the keeper to train them. The small space can cause them agitation and this could cause your pet birds to display frustration and become aggressive to you, it and other cage mates.

Be reminded that these birds, by nature need to be able to spread their wings and fly, survey its horizons from high points in the enclosure and have enough space for their

Chapter Five: Maintenance for Lories and Lorikeets

play and exercise. Both Lory and lorikeet species should be given daily socialization and to form bonds. For an overall well-balanced social life, these birds are recommended to be kept in pairs to keep each other company.

Lories and lorikeets fare well in indoor temperatures not exceeding 80F. Their enclosure must be kept on the floor in a well-lit area away from drafts. A metal grate covering the droppings tray helps keep the bird clean and away from their bodies.

It is essential for these impressively smart birds to make and have full use of all sorts of toys which may and could include natural chew toys, foot toys, luff toys, hanging toys, plastic toys, swings, tiny beams to balance on and the like. The reason why environmental enrichment toys are important is because these in fact literally keep the birds content and happy.

These play items also help stave off aggressive behavior if you what you want is a happy friendly pet and not an angry, frustrated and aggressive monster. It is important to raise your bird in the manner it requires while the birds are young and the brain is still in development. Doing so not only assures you of a mentally and physically sound avian, this measure of preparation and provision will also make for an easier transition for them and a quicker integration into your home.

Cage Maintenance

The specialized diets of nectars and fruit make the droppings of Lories and lorikeets, wet, messy, and colorful. So expect to have messy cages that would need regular maintenance. To avoid their food from being compromised by bird droppings do not place feeding trays under perches or swings. Lories and lorikeets are pretty messy cage residents and seem to randomly poop at will. Make sure you clean out their cages daily to avoid the breeding of bacteria or fungus.

Fecal contamination of its food and water supply is a likely possibility and can be bad for your bird's health if ingested that way. Aside from locating their food and water dishes away from where it bird droppings can be deposited, regularly check the dishes for any signs of discoloration that could likely be an "accident" that happened.

A daily cleaning is required and a fresh sheet of paper to absorb their wet droppings is to be replaced each time you clean their enclosure. Make sure that any metal parts of their enclosure like the hatch and bars are rust free and the

Chapter Five: Maintenance for Lories and Lorikeets

paint is not chipped - a serious health issue for the bird should it get any of the chipped paint in its mouth and swallow the flaked bits.

A thorough cleaning of the cage must be carried out each month using warm water mixed with mild liquid detergent. One part vinegar to eight parts of water is another household solution you can make in your kitchen. The fittings and furnishings of the cage are also to be individually cleaned with the same solution. Before placing the bird back in the enclosure make sure that it has been completely rinsed out.

Make certain that there are no leads, zinc or lead-based paint, or galvanized parts or pieces of the enclosure as all these elements will cause serious harm to your birds if eaten. Make sure that you initially invest well on a cage that will last long, is durable and its parts are free of underlying toxic chemicals that can cause potential harm to your bird. .

When it comes to finding the right cage location, Lories and lorikeets are most of the time too talkative and noisy, that's why you should also take that into consideration when finding a good location for your bird. Put them in a place where they'll get to interact with people, and won't be too much of a disturbance at the same time.

Chapter Five: Maintenance for Lories and Lorikeets

Put the cage at an eye level to create a sense of confidence in your bird and place the cage in a higher location so that they would feel secure just like in the wild.

Avoid placing the cage near dangerous fumes or drafts, this might kill them. Do not also place it directly in a window because the sun can cause your parrot to become ill due to too much heat. If it helps you can at least find a shade or cover for the cage, so that your bird may get just the right amount of heat during the day and feel comfortable during night time.

Finding the right location of the cage could lessen stressful situations for your bird so that they can enjoy their life with their new owner.

Now that your cage is all set and you already have an idea on where to properly place it, you need to provide supplies to meet its needs. Some of its needs include perches, toys, dishes, formulated diets as well as treats.

One of the most important things you need to purchase is perches. The main purpose of perches is to exercise your bird's feet; it could also prevent sores and foot related health issues in the future. In the wild, birds like

Chapter Five: Maintenance for Lories and Lorikeets

lories and lorikeets, are used to transferring from one tree to another but in captivity of course they can't do that, so a great alternative is to buy them perches, preferably made out of fresh fruit tree branches. The minimum area for the perch is about 2 - 2.5 cm in diameter.

You can buy different types of perches such as wood dowel, natural branch type, a therapeutic perch or a cement perch as well as Eucalyptus branches; just make sure that it is not poisonous.

Most parrots also love to gnaw perches, and because of that you may have to replace it regularly. There are lots of perches you could choose from especially from online stores. These perches could also be used as ropes and swings for your pet. Do not put the perch above the bird's bowl or dishes otherwise the food and water will be contaminated.

The next thing are toys, birds in general are very playful and active and like any other birds, they will chew anything, you may find yourself regularly buying and replacing new toys to keep them happy. It is recommended that you purchase toys that are easy to be destroyed, it'll be very interactive for your lories and lorikeets to prevent boredom. However, if you're in a tight budget, you can also buy toys that are durable so that it could last longer.

Chapter Five: Maintenance for Lories and Lorikeets

There are a lot of toys online and in pet stores that you can buy for your parrot. It is not advisable to put all of the toys inside your bird's cage because it will become dirty and overcrowded. Rotate the toys at least once a week.

You should also provide dishes; buy at least 3 sturdy dishes; one for fresh water, one for pellet or seed mix and one for fresh foods. Avoid buying plastic dishes because your lorikeets will most likely break it and it could also be harmful to its health. Place it away from the perches so that it would not be contaminated with bird droppings.

Some parrots owners feed their birds only with seeds, while some only provides a pellet diet; this however could limit the nutrients your pet is receiving. Experts suggest that parrots should be given a variety of food for a balanced nutrition or what they call a formulated diet.

Lories and lorikeets are a very energetic and also a cheerful parrot that's why a good combination of seeds, fruits and vegetables as well as a good amount of protein and other nutrients plus clean water is essential to keep their bodies healthy and active.

You will need a good supply of packaged pellet diet, to be mixed with seed. Then you can slowly add fresh foods

Chapter Five: Maintenance for Lories and Lorikeets

and protein. Formulated bird food may already contain vitamins so it's not recommended that you give another one separately unless prescribed by your vet. Conversion takes about a week or so depending on your bird and how well you feed them.

Aside from formulated diet, Lories and lorikeets can also be taught to perform different kinds of tricks and should undergo "bird training," but of course, it always comes with a price! You can give your pet different types of treats such as fruits, seed and spray as well as Do-It-Yourself (DIY) treats like pretzels, popcorn or something healthy that your bird can munch on. In this book, you will be provided with a list of recommended treats as well as treats you should avoid.

How to Clean Your Parrot

Lories and lorikeets need a regular bath ideally in the morning, to maintain a good skin condition. Here are some things you need to know on how to maintain your bird's hygiene and keep a healthy life; you should provide a misting bottle or a birdbath. All birds should be gently misted with a water bottle at room temperature. The spray should be sprayed up over the bird much like a shower rain, never spray the bird directly in its face.

Chapter Five: Maintenance for Lories and Lorikeets

It's important that you keep an eye in your bird while it is bathing. Bathe your lories with clean water. Distilled water is sometimes required. Speak to your veterinarian on the best choice of water for your bird. During its misting and bathing procedures, make sure there are no drafts because it can cause respiratory issues. It may chill your bird when he is wet. Use towels and blankets, but be careful because it can catch the bird's nails and beaks in their threads.

To ensure that the oils from their skin glands, disease organisms or items such as lotions and hand creams do not transfer to your bird's feathers, wash your hands with soap and water thoroughly before handling your lorikeets.

Your bird may be ill if it seems to stop grooming and becomes dirty. Once you see this signs, contact your avian veterinarian immediately.

Cage Temperature

The average room temperature for your parrots should be anywhere between 18 - 24°C. Also avoid drafty areas that will get direct heat from sun for any portion of the day.

Parrots also have tetra-chromic vision (4 color light vision including ultraviolet), that's why a full color light

Chapter Five: Maintenance for Lories and Lorikeets

bulb must be present in the cage area. The incandescent or monochromatic light bulbs usually found in households are not a good choice for your lories.

Cover the cage during nighttime or at least provide a shade to block out any excess light and also creates a more secure sleeping place. Be careful when using fabrics as cover because your bird might rip it with its claws or beak and could likely eat it.

Never ever place the cage in the kitchen or somewhere near cooking fumes because bird's can be very sensitive, that even a small amount of smoke can be fatal.

Diet and Feeding

Out in the wild the Lory's and Lorikeet's diet is made up of berries, nectar, pollen, fruits and juicy insects. They possess a uniquely distinct and utilitarian tongue which is covered with brush-like papillae and is purposed to gather pollen. The Lory's and lorikeet's ventricular or gizzard of is not strong or sturdy enough to handle a dry seeds-diet or the hard foods other parrots ingest.

This is perhaps why Lories and lorikeets haven't gained fair favor amongst bird keepers as their other parrot cousins

Chapter Five: Maintenance for Lories and Lorikeets

have, and had not caught up with the popularity of other seed eating parrots. Realizing this special diet need of these birds, bird food manufacturers have created commercially produced powder and nectar diets were formulated specifically for Lories and lorikeets.

Now, the once challenging and difficult feeding process of this gaily-colored avifauna is no longer the hurdle it once was. A diet made up of a high quality Lory/lorikeet food along with a medley of fresh and crispy fruits and vegetables as well as regular replenishment of fresh, clean water should take care of keeping your bird happy and healthy.

Do not make the mistake of feeding your Lories and/or lorikeets foods that do not provide them nutritional value. Doing so could lead to malnourishment and starvation. If not given the proper sort of food they need malnourishment can cause their immune system to weaken thereby making them vulnerable to worse medical conditions.

With the advent of specialized foods specifically made for lories and lorikeets there is no reason for a bird to be given any other substitute foods that may not sit well with the bird or at worst cause it to fall ill.

Chapter Five: Maintenance for Lories and Lorikeets

Nutritional Needs of Lories and Lorikeets

If you are an existing Lory and/or Lorikeet keeper then you already know the delicate balance that needs to be maintained in relation to your feathered-pal's special diet needs.

If you are a potential and future Lory and/or Lorikeet guardian then you need to be aware that your soon-to-join-the-family-ranks pet bird needs specific type of bird grub. On the discussion of your bird's proper nutrition there is no one-type-fits-all.

Your soon to be feathered-companion has limited food choices that can not to be taken lightly or disregarded. Your colorful avifauna-buddy imperatively needs a specific and certain sort of Lory/Lorikeet bird diet. Be mindful to take note of what you can and shouldn't serve your soon to move in chatty roommate.

Provide them with high quality nectar produced commercially or a specialized pellet diet. Supplement this with finely chopped fruits and vegetables mixed in with baby food and a tiny amount of fortified seeds.

Chapter Five: Maintenance for Lories and Lorikeets

Provide and replenish fresh water in their enclosure daily and make sure that their water dish is kept away from hanging swings and perches to avoid feces from contaminating the water. Do not feed them sugary or treat containing a fat.

Types of Food

The literally colorful and comical Lory/Lorikeet is a talented tight-rope artist and acrobat who is playfully active. The seemingly constant activities of the bird will surely work up quite an appetite in it and will almost certainly demand to be fed. Aside from its specialized diet of pollen, nectar, fruits, insects, vegetables, etc., a keeper will also need to mind that the Lory/Lorikeet is given a diet meant for medium sized birds.

Diet mixes suitable for the Lory and Lorikeet is and will be a fantastic pantry-staple to have on hand for when you are too busy or don't have enough time to prepare a kitchen mix of goodies. You want to remember that offering a variety of fresh foods like fruits, and vegetables along with its favorite staples of pollen, insects and nectar (amongst some of its allowed food) is absolutely necessary for your bird's nutritional health and wellness.

Chapter Five: Maintenance for Lories and Lorikeets

It means that you will have to limit the serving of food mixes and save this for hectic-scheduled days. Pelleted diets are produced by mixing a selection of nutritionally sound ingredients (safe for your Lory) into a mash which is then formed to various pellet sizes. Bird pellets provide a better balanced parrot diet nutritional for your bird. The convenience of serving pellets as a base for the rest of the Loris' required diet is breeze and reduces the likelihood of your bird picking through the healthier components of its food which it really needs. However, do not make the mistake of serving this alone as it will not satisfy the nutritional needs of your Lory. Most vegetables and fruits can be served to your Lory.

Here is a short list of greens and fruits you can serve up to your Lorikeet. As when you prepare your meals, do not forget to wash the produce well. These foods listed below can be given in any form available; boiled, canned, fresh, frozen unless indicated otherwise

- Soybeans
- Spinach (in moderation)
- Sprouts
- Squash (i.e. acorn, butternut, Hubbard, etc.)
- Sweet potatoes (cooked)

Chapter Five: Maintenance for Lories and Lorikeets

- Thai pepper
- Tomatoes (cooked and dried)
- Watercress
- Yams (cooked)
- Bamboo shoots
- Banana peppers
- Beans (cooked) (i.e. adzuki, butter, garbanzo, green, haricot, kidney, mango, navy, pinto, pole, soy, wax, etc.)
- Bean sprouts
- Beets
- Bell peppers
- Broccoli
- Broccoli flower
- Cabbage
- Carrots (including tops)
- Cauliflower
- Cayenne
- Celery

It is up to you now to do in-depth research on other kinds of vegetables acceptable to serve your Lory. Fruits are fantastic sources of all kinds of vitamins. Be sure that you provide your Lory a variety of these fruits for its optimum health-advantage

Chapter Five: Maintenance for Lories and Lorikeets

- Dates
- Figs
- Guava
- Honeydew (no rinds)
- Mangoes
- Passion fruit
- Lychee
- Lemons
- Loquat
- Mandarin oranges
- Kumquats
- Nectarines (remove pit and area around the pit)
- Oranges
- Papaya
- Raisins
- Apples (remove seeds and stem)
- Cherimoya
- Tangerines
- Blueberries
- Clementine oranges
- Pomegranate
- Kiwis
- Grapefruit
- Cantaloupe (no rinds)
- Plantains
- Grapes (i.e. black, green, red, etc.)

Chapter Five: Maintenance for Lories and Lorikeets

- Peaches (remove pit and area around the pit)
- Pears (remove seeds)
- Pineapple
- Plums (remove pit and area around the pit)
- Apricots (remove pit and area around the pit)
- Bananas (remove peel)
- Blackberries
- Cactus fruit
- Cherries (no pits)
- Coconuts
- Cranberries
- Currants

Toxic Foods to Avoid

Just as other animals that have zero tolerance for some kinds of foods in terms of ingestion, digestion and processing, so is your Lory/Lorikeet. There are a number of foods and liquids they should not be given or offered or you could ultimately be the cause of the bird falling ill - or worse. Do not attempt to give your bird the following:

- Fruit pits and the flesh around them (contain cyanide)
- Rhubarb
- Chocolate
- Alcohol

Chapter Five: Maintenance for Lories and Lorikeets

- Avocado
- Caffeine

Handling and Training Lories and Lorikeets

First off, a novice keeper importantly needs to understand that a seemingly stubborn Lory is a basic bird trait and is normal. It doesn't understand you yet. Your Lorikeet just needs some time, like anyone else, learning to speak a language. So give both yourselves a break and keep at it with willingness and a goal. Training your Lory will not be the easiest task to undertake and can oftentimes cause frustration. Don't let your impatience get the best of you.

You will soon discover that if you create your private shout-out call, your Lorikeet will begin to answer back. Practice this habit when you're in a separate area of your home and your buddy-bird makes a noise - do it by responding to that call.

The Lory is a social bird (in the literal sense) and is probably checking out what's keeping you when you are clearly at home! "Shout-out" back to your feathered companion and let them know that you are just a wall away. Making up your own special shout-out call not only makes

Chapter Five: Maintenance for Lories and Lorikeets

for good bonding with your Lory, this also helps it understand the words out of your mouth little by little.

How to Tame Your Lories and Lorikeets

Taming your colorful and sometimes witty lories/lorikeets is the first thing to do before teaching them some cool tricks. The only flipside in owning a this kind of bird is that they have quite a reputation for being a bit mischievous, in some cases they even tend to bite when they feel threatened. It is essential to figure out the level of your bird's comfort zone and remove it so that you could have a great bonding experience together.

The first step is to slowly touch your parrot in its beak, then carefully move your hand closer and closer towards its beak. If the parrot reacts or moves away, stop for a while. Wait for it to calm down, then take your hand away and give a treat. Practice repeating this procedure until you is able to fully touch its beak. Your lories will eventually tolerate you in touching its beak and once you do, you can also scratch their beak. Just be extra careful when doing it, their beaks are sharp and really strong, but you have to conquer your fear if you want to get along with them.

Chapter Five: Maintenance for Lories and Lorikeets

Once you and your Lories get along already, strengthen your relationship by training them some basic lessons. Training a parrot in general is not that hard to do, in fact it can be a fun and rewarding bonding experience for you and your feathered friend. There are lots of pet owners out there who have properly trained and raised well-behaved lorikeets. They are smart creatures by nature, that is why they can absorb information very quickly and easily as long as you do it right. Trust is the most important key in training your parrot or any other pet for that matter. The first thing you need to do is to be able to establish a solid connection and rapport between you and your pet.

One of the basic skills that your parrot needs to learn is stepping – up. It's a good way to pacify your bird into your hands without being forceful is to try and make your parakeet step up onto a handheld perch. Slowly and progressively begin training it to step up on your hand. If you are afraid of being bitten then wear gloves, but you may want to get rid of it eventually because it might still encourage them to bite you because they can chew the leather. Hold your hand in a short distance away from your parrot so that when it tries to step into the target stick, it will have no choice but to step into your hand. Keep practicing until your parrot won't need your stick anymore. It will get

Chapter Five: Maintenance for Lories and Lorikeets

accustomed and comfortable whenever you command it to step up in your finger

Grooming Your Lories and Lorikeets

Grooming your Lories and lorikeets involves trimming your nails, beaks as well as its wings. First stop is your parrot's nails, however, before attempting to trim the nails of your Lories and Lorikeets you will want to learn how to do this procedure by watching an expert do it. The best candidate for this job is your avian vet who can assist you in learning the procedure.

By no means should a keeper carry out this task on their own if they are unsure, unconfident and prone to nervousness. The bird will sense your hesitation and anxiety and may struggle to break free of your hold. Like many parrots, Lories and lorikeets have a sharp, needle-like nails because they do a lot of climbing in the wild, and they also use these nails to dig into wood to keep them secure.

Unclipped nails can dig into the skin, leaving scratches or painful wounds to a person, only clipped to a point that the bird can perch securely and does not bother you when the bird is perched on your hand. Many people have their bird's nails clipped to the point that it becomes dull and the bird can no longer grip a perch firmly, this can

Chapter Five: Maintenance for Lories and Lorikeets

result to becoming more clumsy and nervous because it cannot move without slipping. This nervousness can develop into fear biting and panic attacks. Another tip is only use a styptic powder on your bird's nails and not its skin.

Although, most parrots can maintain its beak's from deformity on its own, it's still important that you keep them in good condition. They are very fond of chewing and pecking everything they can get into. That's why it may eventually become dull which could also lead to deformation if not properly cared for.

Consult a qualified veterinarian to show you the proper way in trimming your pet's beaks. You can also check out several grooming items such as lava and mineral blocks that are available in your local pet store, to keep their beaks in great shape.

When it comes to clipping its wings, Birds are design to fly, young parrots can be fairly clumsy and flying gives them confidence as well as agility, stamina, and muscle tone but before clipping their wings, make sure that your Lories are flying, maneuvering and landing well already.

Chapter Five: Maintenance for Lories and Lorikeets

If they do not learn how to properly land by lifting their wings and flaring their tail, then when they are clipped, they could injure themselves and could also break their beak or keel bone.

Consult a qualified veterinarian to show you the proper way in clipping a bird's wings. A certain amount of flight feathers will be removed while leaving the smaller balancing feathers inside the wing closer to the body uncut.

Chapter Six: Breeding Lories and Lorikeets

If you are interested in breeding your Lories and lorikeets, this chapter will give you a lot of information about the processes and phases of its breeding and you will also learn how to properly breed them on your own. This is not for everyone but if you want to have better understanding about how these birds procreate, then consider reading this chapter. We will give you some basic breeding info about Lories and lorikeets as well as its breeding process including hybridization.

Chapter Six: Breeding Lories and Lorikeets

Basic Lories and Lorikeets Breeding Info

Any potential keeper guardian of Lories and lorikeets will have to get specific information with regard to the breeding and breeding habits of each particular species or at the very least, breeding information regarding members of the same bird genus. A variety of different species of Lories and lorikeets have been successfully bred in captivity, in aviaries as well as in privately owned enclosures.

Keeper guardians of Lories and lorikeets often wonder if they can and should breed their pet birds. Serious and avid aviculturists are in fact encouraged to breed and allow their captive pets to reproduce. Given that pet Lories and lorikeets are provided with all necessary requirements to breeding readiness, there should be nothing to stop the bird keeper guardian from allowing the natural to happen.

It is but wise to seek the help of a Lory and lorikeet breeder who has had many years of breeding experience and has been highly successful in breeding this colorful duo of impressively intelligent birds. Seek the guidance of experienced breeders and longtime Lory and lorikeet keeper guardians who will be willing to share best practices that worked for them. Best do this - build your Lory and lorikeet breeder/keeper network early - before attempting to carry

Chapter Six: Breeding Lories and Lorikeets

out the breeding process on your own to save you the frustration of inexperience.

Collaborate and get the insights of an experienced Lory and lorikeet breeder who will be able to and willing to discuss effective methods they have successfully employed themselves. Do your own research and gather as much information as you can to give you the confidence to breed your pet birds. Learning how to breed your pet birds effectively will allow you to know what signs to look out for and recognize.

You will also want to seek the advice and assistance of an expert avian veterinarian not only on breeding methods but more importantly on sexing lories and lorikeets. DNA testing has replaced the invasive surgical procedure of sexing Lories and lorikeets. The process is simple, quick and painless

The Lories and Lorikeets Breeding Process

Provided that Lories and lorikeets in captivity are raised in an optimum environment and are provided with a balanced diet, these birds should have no difficulty breeding. Lories and lorikeets are able to reproduce anytime

Chapter Six: Breeding Lories and Lorikeets

of the year. Here are some tips with a good probability of successful and regular breeding.

A true pair isn't necessarily a guarantee that these birds will breed. Perfect pairings are likelier to breed and breed successfully if both birds finds each other interesting and worthy of the others affections. To determine this, you will want to place bird couples in a shared enclosure and observe their reactions to each other. Should there be no reaction to each other within the week of housing them together, provide the *hen* with another mate.

If you are worried about unwarranted attacks to each other, an alternative method to observe the pair together is to place each bird in separate enclosures adjacent to each other and observe their reactions to each other for a period of 7 - 10 days.

Lory and lorikeet pairs which have made no attempt to breed with each other should be separated and introduced to new partners. Often when new partners are introduced, results come soon after.

Lories and lorikeets have very low tolerance for each other and could result in an all-out battle for territory and space if forced to live together. Employ the methods of

Chapter Six: Breeding Lories and Lorikeets

pairing suggested above in this chapter when breeding these parrot sorts to avoid bloody war.

Sometimes paired birds are placed together in an attempt to have the two avifauna breed, only to fail in the attempt. A possible reason for nonbreeding pairs could be that both are of the same sex or possibly two separate species of *loriinae*.

To increase the chances of getting the birds in the mood provide the pair a nest box closely similar to the nests in which they were raised. If this is detail is unknown to you, you may get in touch with the breeder from whom you purchased your birds and ask. If this option turns up without an answer, then let the birds decide by providing the breeding pair a couple of nest boxes you've researched that aren't only suitable but aid in the likelihood of a successful pairing.

Use nest boxes fashioned out of hollow wood from natural tree limbs. Alternatively, a keeper guardian can also use thick planks of wood with appropriate dimensions and isn't too small. Not having enough space to move about in the nest could cause the incubating bird to accidentally damage their eggs or cause injury to their offspring. When the eggs hatch, the growing birds will soon need space and

Chapter Six: Breeding Lories and Lorikeets

the absence of it could be the cause of weaker birds getting crushed or suffocated.

Another provision that must be provided for the breeding pair would be a few or more wooden perches attached firmly to the enclosure to avoid the perches from wobbling. In fact, in the wild most mating happen on perches where birds can socialize with each other.

Place the hen in another aviary and have the male join her a week later, after she has gotten familiar with the new space. She will need to familiarize herself first with ll the furnishings and fitting of the new enclosure. Allow her time to get to know where everything is before the male joins her. In case of a mating gone awry, the female will know where to retreat.

As keeper guardian, you will want to make sure that there is nothing that could cause injury or danger to either bird. Clipping the nails of both birds before pairing them up in the same enclosure, minimizes the chances of injury to either bird. You will want to start experimenting on good pair ups ahead of time and not right just before the breeding process begins. The birds will need to get to know each other and like each other foremost and as keeper it will be up to you to recognize a successful pair up.

Chapter Six: Breeding Lories and Lorikeets

To promote breeding, the birds will need peace and quiet. Disturbing them or the enclosure at this time is strongly discouraged. When approaching the enclosure or nest box housing the pair, make your presence known before hand and speak to them in low, soothing tones. Doing so will allow the birds reassurance of your presence and they may even greet you as you approach. Offer them tidbits of fruits, or mealworms when you pay them a visit to better gain their confidence and trust.

Keep the breeding pair in a temperature controlled space using a broad spectrum light and provide them with a generous supply of tree twigs throughout the breeding period

Hybridization of Lories and Lorikeets

There are breeders who produce hybrids with the intent of introducing new color schemes not normally found in their sort. This purposeful breeding has resulted in some astoundingly brilliant variations of the very well-known Lory and lorikeet breeds. A lot of breeders around the world but especially those in Australia have begun advertising new color variations like the Lutina, Mustard, Cinnamon Rainbows, Yellow and Red-Collared lories and lorikeets.

Chapter Six: Breeding Lories and Lorikeets

Hybrids of Lories are the result of a variety of Lories which are crossbred. A majority of breeders consider this practice unacceptable due to the unnatural Lory produced that is very unlikely to occur in the wild.

With that said, hybridization can and does take place in nature. Some examples have been reported from Australia where a variety of Lories, those that typically share the same geographic location, sources of food and who flock together have been noted to interbreed to produce hybrids which naturally occur.

Examples of this natural occurrence of wild inter breeding are the pairing of Rainbow lorikeets/Scaly-breasted lorikeets, Scaly-breasted lorikeets/Musk lorikeets and Rainbow lorikeets/Red Collared lorikeets.

However, due to hybrid lories having a lower success rate of producing fertile eggs, the effect of the hybrid eventually being bred out over several generations is quite likely to happen, as these birds partner up with normal mates. Survival will also be challenging for these hybrids that are much easier for predators to single out. It is safe to assume that these naturally occurring hybrids will disappear in the future.

Chapter Seven: Keeping Lories and Lorikeets Healthy

Determining the exact cause of illness in a sick Lory and lorikeets can be difficult to recognize or determine because a lot of these bird maladies manifest showing similar symptoms to other illnesses. As earlier mentioned, the potential keeper guardian of Lories and lorikeets should have already gotten in touch with an expert avian vet who specializes in bird health.

The potential keeper should also investigate and find out if there are any underlying causes which are the cause of

Chapter Seven: Keeping Lories and Lorikeets Healthy

the problem. Some problems are stress, draft in the enclosure, boredom, improper diet, amongst other things. This bird sort when not given the opportunity or attention to get enough exercise, social interaction and mental stimulation can fall into deep depression thereby harming their immune system and making them candidates to be succumb easier to maladies.

Gentle mist grooming and hygiene must be done daily using a spray bottle exclusively for misting your birds. Birds are frequent bathers and this is one way of making sure they get their daily bath. You can also place a crock of water which will double as bird bath two times a week.

Take your Lories and lorikeets to your avian vet for a regular trimming of wings and nails. The wings of Lories and lorikeets can be conservatively be trimmed thereby curbing the possibility of injury - and escape.

Be sure to bring your Lories and lorikeets to the avian vet you trust for an annual physical exam to make certain that all is working well and the bird is healthy and physically sound.

Chapter Seven: Keeping Lories and Lorikeets Healthy

Common Health Problems

Just like any other pet a potential guardian/keeper wishes to acquire, Lories and lorikeets too have their own special needs for which they will need provisions. The birds will also have their own restrictions and adverse reactions which a keeper should be aware of to avoid this avifauna from falling ill.

Much like other animals and pets, Lories and lorikeets also have their weaknesses and can be prone to some illnesses more than other parrots are. It is important that the potential keeper guardian of these birds empower themselves with informative, medical conditions and recognize, if not suspect, symptoms of illnesses in their birds to be able to seek medical attention quickly.

Some common health issues Lories and lorikeets are susceptible to are Chlamydiosis and Psittacine of the beak and its feathers.

Chlamydiosis is silently indicated when there is loss of appetite, a display of feathers that are fluffed and by nasal discharge.

Chapter Seven: Keeping Lories and Lorikeets Healthy

Psittacine of the feathers and beak is indicated with a loss of feathers, abnormal coloration of the feathers and abnormalities of the beak. For these two conditions the keeper guardian will want to seek immediate avian vet attention.

Other medical conditions these birds can experience would be nutritional deficiencies due to improper diet and the absence of their staple food of nectar, pollen, flowers, as well as supplemental powder and pellets made specifically to meet their nutritional needs.

Lories are specifically vulnerable to iron storage disease and must not be given iron in its diet which exceeds more than 100 parts per million

Beak and feather disease in birds is an air-borne aviary disease that is highly contagious. As keeper guardian, you will want to discuss this condition further with your avian vet to find out how this happens, what you can do in the unfortunate event that it does, and steps needed to be taken.

You'll find some useful information in this portion of the book that will reveal more of what you can do, what you

Chapter Seven: Keeping Lories and Lorikeets Healthy

should look out for and steps you need to take in order to keep your Lory and lorikeet in the pink of health.

Recommended Tests

Ask the breeder of your feathered friends what sort of tests they have given to the Lories and lorikeets. Make sure that the medical information, if they indeed have given the Lories and lorikeets physical exams, are recorded, and given to for you to file away in a medical file for each of the birds in question.

You will need to make a trip to the avian vet with your Lories and lorikeets before taking them home to have the vet give them a clean bill of health. The avian vet would be the best person to determine the health and wellness of your birds.

Other tests your trusted avian vet may tell you that your lories and lorikeets should get is preventive and to annually check that its health is stable and uncompromised. Below are other preventive medicine exams you may wish to ask your avian vet about.

Ask about an annual physical examination. The first one may be scheduled on the day you bring your bird's

Chapter Seven: Keeping Lories and Lorikeets Healthy

home with you. A yearly exam is recommended for all birds. You will want to obtain and establish a baseline data of regular clinical testing's such as a complete blood count (CBC), plasma biochemistries and protein electrophoresis.

As mentioned earlier you will not want to take your Lories and lorikeets straight home and quarantine is strongly advised for novice keepers to heed. Your avian vet will inform you of how long the quarantine will last. As excited as you are to bring home your new friends, this is a necessary measure of safety and prevention that will benefit all parties positively.

Hemolytic anemia in Lories may occur if your Lories are given the equine West Nile virus vaccine. Ask your vet about the necessity of this vaccine and take it from there.

Based on history, specific diseases and physical exam results there is a chance that the vet recommend further exams for avian chlamydiosis and avian polyomavirus.

There is a higher risk of Pacheco's disease virus amongst birds housed in aviaries or large groups. Your vet will be able to best determine if your lories and lorikeets should be vaccinated.

Chapter Seven: Keeping Lories and Lorikeets Healthy

For Lories and lorikeets that are part of a group of breeding avian the avian polyomavirus vaccine will likely be recommended by your vet.

Signs of Possible Illnesses

Look out for red flags that may indicate an unhealthy lory/lorikeet. It is up to the keeper guardian of the birds to be able to identify when a bird displays behavior that could be early signs of illnesses as well as know what unusual physical conditions to look out for that give warning of a sick bird.

- Swelling of the beak
- Sitting on base of enclosure
- Coughing and or wheezing
- The bird sneezes more than occasionally
- Fluffed, soiled and plucked feathers
- Ruffled plumage
- Normal luster of plumage is lost
- Bare spots on the plumage
- Stools that are discolored or runny
- It favors one foot over the other
- Swollen or red eyes
- Nasal or eye discharge
- A loss of appetite

Chapter Seven: Keeping Lories and Lorikeets Healthy

- Not drinking water
- Other unusual symptoms

Should you notice any of these signs in any of your future pet birds, you will first want to gently take them out of their usual enclosure and isolate them from the rest (if you are acquiring more than one of them) to make sure that there is no contamination of healthy birds. It is important before acquisition of the birds for the keeper guardian, to have gotten in touch with and partner up with a good avian vet because your birds will sooner or later need the expertise and services of one.

Chapter Eight: Lories and Lorikeet in Summary

Now that you have come to the end of this book, we trust that you have more knowledge of the beautifully plumed, colorful, friendly, playful, docile, can sometimes be aggressive and territorial lories and lorikeets. Here are some reminders to take away before you go on your quest to find the perfect Lory and lorikeet you want to share your home with.

Chapter Eight: Lories and Lorikeets in Summary

Your commitments to raising these birds are not limited to changing their water dishes and filling their feeding bowls. Your presence and attention is almost demanded by Lories and lorikeets and the absence of your companionship can cause them depression and problematic behavior changes like constant screeching. Be sure you allot the required amount of time to spend with your birds to help them exercise, train them to do tricks, bathe them, and talk to them

Remember to deal only with breeders who are willing and ready to answer questions about the bird. Ask about its origin, how it was bred, when it was bred and the method of their breeding program.

You will want to have an experienced avian vet to consult with and to bring your bird to for yearly physical exams. Network with seasoned Lories and lorikeet keeper guardians as they can be a reliable ally for times when you need confirmation, advice or suggestions on how to raise your birds effectively.

Make sure that you have all the feeding equipment's, enclosure, furnishings, fittings and playthings for your Lories and lorikeets. Be sure to have a sufficient supply of food for your birds as well.

Chapter Eight: Lories and Lorikeets in Summary

Most of all prepare yourself for a new world of companionship with the amusingly comical, entertainer who will soon be joining ranks in your home.

Basic Information

- **Taxonomy:** phylum *Chordata*, class *Aves*, order *Psittaciformes*, family *Psittaculidae*, Subfamily *Loriinae*, Tribe *Loriini*
- **Distribution**: Asia, Polynesia, Papua New Guinea, Timor Leste, and Australia
- **Habitat**: Scrublands, Woodlands, Grasslands
- **Lifestyle**: Flock Oriented
- **Anatomical Adaptations**:
- **Breeding Season**: between November to February
- **Eggs**: 3 – 6 eggs
- **Incubation Period**: 21 - 25 days
- **Sexual Maturity** : 6 – 7 months old
- **Average Size**: 16 – 15 inches
- **Average Weight**: 50 – 300 grams
- **Wingspan**: 140 – 151 mm
- **Coloration**: Lorikeets are usually green with patches of yellow and red; Lories have a red body with patches of purple, green and yellow
- **Sexual Dimorphism**: Sexually dimorphic

Chapter Eight: Lories and Lorikeets in Summary

- **Diet**: Seeds, Insects, Fruit, Nuts (Omnivore)
- **Sounds:** Vocal Communicator
- **Interaction:** Highly Social
- **Lifespan**: 13 – 25 years

Cage Set-up Guide

- **Minimum Cage Dimensions**: 36"x 48"x 24"
- **Bar Spacing**: not more than 0.5 in (1.3 cm)
- **Required Accessories**: food and water dishes, perches, grooming and cleaning materials, toys
- **Food/Water Dish**: sturdy dishes; one for fresh water, one for pellet/seed mix, and one for fresh foods. Do not buy dishes made out of plastic
- **Perches**: at least 3 different perches; wood dowel, natural branch type, a therapeutic perch or a cement perch or any fresh fruit tree branches
- **Recommended Toys**: rotate at least 3 different toys; rope toys, stainless steel bells, swings etc.
- **Bathing Materials**: misting bottle; bath tub
- **Nests Materials**: nest box made out of wood, oak or metal
- **Recommended Temperature Range**: 65-75°F (18 - 24°C) or not exceeding 80°F

Chapter Eight: Lories and Lorikeets in Summary

- **Lighting:** full color light bulb must be present in the cage area. Do not use incandescent or monochromatic light bulbs.

Nutritional Information

- **Types of Recommended Food:**
- **Seeds:** 1/8 - 1/4 cup of fortified parrot seed mix
- **Fresh Fruits and Vegetables:** Offer fruits and vegetables daily or every 2 - 3 days.
- **Supplements:** Calcium usually found in the form of a cuttlebone or Calcium treat.
- **Amino Acids:** makes up about 20% of a Lorie's diet.
- **Carbohydrates:** makes up about 10% of a Lorie's diet
- **Water:** clean, fresh and cool water; unflavored bottled drinking water or bottled natural spring water

Breeding Information

- **Sexual Dimorphism**: They are sexually dimorphic; gender can be identified through DNA sexing or chromosomal analysis as well as body shape and length
- **Seasonal Changes**: breeding season usually begins in from November to February.
- **Sexual Maturity:** 6 – 7 months old
- **Nest Box Size:** 16" x 16" x 8"

Chapter Eight: Lories and Lorikeets in Summary

- **Egg Laying**: female lays eggs an average of 3 – 6 eggs or more.
- **Clutch Size**: about 2 - 3 clutches per year or more
- **Incubation Period**: 21 - 25 days
- **Hatching**: takes about 24 – 48 hours to hatch
- **Chick Independence:** 1 – 2 months (50 - 60 days)

Chapter Nine: Breeder Referrals and Relevant Websites

In this chapter we will provide you with some links on where you can buy supplies such as food and cage accessories so that it can save you time and effort. You might also want to compare prices, brands, and its quality before purchasing. The links given here are some of the most popular and recommended websites by pet owners, avian experts and enthusiasts. Check them out so you can also decide what will fit on your budget. We also provided a list of other several breeders and sellers of Lories and lorikeets.

Local Lories and Lorikeets Breeders in the United States

Chapter Nine: Relevant Websites

Here are the lists of available Lories and Lorikeet breeders in the United States. Availability and costs of these birds may vary over time, please check the links provided for any updates.

CALIFORNIA
Dick Schroeder
San Marcos, CA - 810 North Twin Oaks Valley Road, #131, San Marcos, CA 92069
Phone: 760- 591-4951

Ginos Exiotic Birds
Blue Jay, CA 92317
Website: http://www.birdbreeders.com/bird
Tel. No.: 176-095-604-66
Email: Gmorrialle@gmail.com

Thea's Parrot Place
Fallbrook, California 92028
Website: www.theasparrotplace.com
Tel. No.: 760-842-3436
Email: theasparrotplace@att.net

Ara Aviaries California
Agoura Hills Los Angeles, California
Website: www.aracaris.com
Tel. No.: 805-338-3549
Email: billysaylors6@gmail.com

Chapter Nine: Relevant Websites

The Parrot's Cove
New Iberia, Los Angeles 70560
Website: theparrotcove.com
Tel. No.: 337-519-3943
E-mail: theparrotscove@theparrotcove.com

Toucan Jungle
Vista, CA 92084
Website: www.ToucanJungle.com
Tel. No.: 760-672-0127
Email: Chris@Toucanjungle.com

FLORIDA

Lory Website

http://www.lorywebsite.com/

Featherheads
Port charlotte, Florida 33948
Website:http://www.birdbreeders.com/breeder/13627/featherheads-florida-port-charlotte-FL
Tel. No.: 813-679-4961

Linville's Aviary
Miami, Florida 33174
Website:http://www.birdbreeders.com/breeder/2920/linvilles-aviary-miami-FL
Tel. No.: 305-968-1536
E-mail: cerbyu@aol.com

Chapter Nine: Relevant Websites

Lone Palm Aviary
Loxahatchee, Florida 33470
Website: www.lpbirds.com
Tel. No.: 570-730-1366
Email: jessica@lpbirds.com

The Finch Farm Co.
Miami, Florida 33101
Website: www.thefinchfarm.com
Tel. No.: 877-527-5656
E-mail: jenna.thefinchfarm@gmail.com

IOWA

Zimmerman Pet's - located in N.W Iowa (Sioux City, IA)
Tel. 712-239-5531

NEW JERSEY

Marie Hageman
Sewell, NJ
Tel.: 609-589-0606

World of Birds
15 Perry Street, Chester, New Jersey 07930
Website: www.worldofbirds.com
Tel. No.: 908-879-2291
Email: worldofbirds@optonline.net

Fancy Feathers

Chapter Nine: Relevant Websites

31 Roseland Avenue, Caldwell, New Jersey
Website: www.fancyfeathersaviary.com
Tel. No.: 973-403-2900
E-mail: ddargenio@gmail.com

Birds Exotic

1060 S. Chester Ave. Delran, NJ 08075
Website: www.thebirdstore.com
Tel. No.: 856-764-2473
E-mail: thebirdstore@yahoo.com

OREGON

The Parrot Patch Aviary - located in Eugene, Oregon - Contact Tom Sauer
Tel. 541-463-9564

Cage Links

Here is the recommended list of websites for you to choose from when buying cages both in United States and Great Britain.

Custom Cages
<https://www.customcages.com >

Bird Cages 4 Less

Chapter Nine: Relevant Websites

<http://birdcages4less.com/page/B/CTGY/Small_Bird_Cages>

Bird Cages Now

<http://www.birdcagesnow.com>

Pet Solutions

<http://www.petsolutions.com/C/Bird-Cages-Carriers.aspx>

Pets at Home

<http://www.petsathome.com/shop/en/pets/bird-and-wildlife/bird-cages>

Overstock

<http://www.overstock.com/Pet-Supplies/Bird-Cages-Houses/3643/cat.html>

Cages World

<http://www.cagesworld.co.uk>

Northern Parrots

<http://www.northernparrots.com>

Pebble – Home and Garden

Chapter Nine: Relevant Websites

<https://www.pebble.co.uk>

Seapets

<https://www.seapets.co.uk/bird-supplies/bird-cages/parrot-cages>

Cage Accessories and Supplies

Here is the recommended list of websites for you to choose from when buying accessories such as toys, perches, dishes and other necessary supplies for your pet.

King's Cages

<http://www.kingscages.com/>

Doctors Foster and Smith – Toys

<http://www.drsfostersmith.com/bird-supplies/>

Fun Time Birdy - Toys

<http://www.funtimebirdy.com/patoyse.html>

Pet Mountain – Cleaning Supplies

Chapter Nine: Relevant Websites

< http://www.petmountain.com/category/311/1/bird-cage-cleaning-supplies.html>

PetSmart – Bowls, Feeders

<http://www.petsmart.com/bird/bowls-feeders/cat-36-catid-400014>

Wind City Parrot - Accessories

<http://www.windycityparrot.com/All_c_711.html>

Pet Solutions - Breeding Supplies

<http://www.petsolutions.com/C/Bird-Breeding-Supplies.aspx>

Bird Cages 4 Less - Perches

<http://birdcages4less.com/page/B/CTGY/Bird_Perches>

Pets at Home – Health Care Products

<http://www.petsathome.com/shop/en/pets/bird-and-wildlife/bird-healthcare-products>

Overstock - Accessories

<http://www.overstock.com/Pet-Supplies/Bird-Accessories/3646/cat.html>

Diet and Food Links

Chapter Nine: Relevant Websites

Here is the recommended list of websites for you to choose from when buying seeds and parrot food for your pet.

Harrison's Bird Food
<http://www.harrisonsbirdfoods.com/>

Nature Chest - Bird Food
<http://www.naturechest.com/bifoforinri.html>

Petco – Bird Food; Treats
<http://www.petco.com/shop/en/petcostore/bird/bird-food-and-treats>

Pet Supplies Plus
<http://www.petsuppliesplus.com/thumbnail/Bird/Food-Treats/c/2142/2162.uts>

That Pet Place – Bird Food Supplies
<http://www.thatpetplace.com/bird-supplies/bird-food#!bird-food>

Scarletts Parrot Essentials UK – Bird Food
<http://www.scarlettsparrotessentials.co.uk/food>

Seapets – Bird Food

Chapter Nine: Relevant Websites

<https://www.seapets.co.uk/bird-supplies/bird-food/bird-seeds>

ZooPlus
<http://www.zooplus.co.uk/shop/birds/bird_food/parrot>

Bird Food UK
<http://www.birdfood.co.uk/ctrl/node:114;page:2;/bird_foods>

Ideal Price UK
<http://www.idealprice.co.uk>

Northern Parrots – Parrot Treatments
<http://www.northernparrots.com/treatments-and-cures-dept139/>

Glossary

Abdomen - bottom part of the bird

Alula - three feathers springing from the base of the primaries

Addled eggs - These eggs are not viable and will not hatch.

Afterfeather - A structure that projects from the shaft of the feather at the rim of the superior umbilicus.

Allopreening - An act of social grooming amongst birds, in which one bird preens the other or a pair of birds does so mutually.

Alternate plumage - The plumage of birds displayed in time for courtship or a breeding season.

Altricial - hatchlings with their eyes closed, and are not capable of leaving the nest on its own, and rely on parents for food.

Alula - a bird's "thumb"

Anisodactylus - a bird foot which has three toes pointing forward and one toe pointing at the back

Anting - a behavior when birds rub insects, typically ants, on their feathers and skin

Aviculture - captive breeding and rising of birds

Abdomen - bottom part of the bird

Axillary - ventral area between the body and the wing

Back - exterior area of a bird's upper parts between its mantle and rump

Basic plumage - non-breeding plumage

Beak - bill or rostrum

Beak trimming - the partial removal of the beak

Belly - the area beneath the chest of a bird

Billing - a tendency of mated pairs that strengthen couple bonding

Bird banding - a tag attached to the leg of a bird to enable identification

Bird strike - bird/s that impact with planes in flight

Body down - soft, down feathers underneath bird's outer feathers.

Breast - body part between throat and belly

Breeding plumage - plumage displayed by birds during breeding season

Brood - offspring birds

Brood patch - an area of bare skin well supplied with blood vessels at the surface, and facilitates the transfer of heat to the eggs

Call - bird vocalization intending to serve as warning alarm

Cloaca - birds expel waste from it; other mate by joining cloaca; females lay eggs from this region

Contact call - to make known to their kind the location of a bird

Crissum - feathered area between the vent and the tail

Cryptic plumage - plumage meant to camouflage birds

Definitive plumage - plumage completely developed and fixed

Down - the softest of the birds feathers

Egg - where birds develop until hatched

Egg incubation - act of warming the eggs to promote hatching

Eye-ring - visible ring of feathers surrounding a bird's eyes

Feather - distinct outer "garment" covering a birds' body

Feather pecking - a behavioral problem when one bird repeatedly pecks at the feathers of another bird

Fledge - a young bird that completely develops its wing muscles and feather suitable for flight

Fledgling - the period when a completely formed young bird ventures out of the nest and learns to take flight

Flight - the act of soaring in the air with the use of wings

Gizzard - specialized stomach organ found in the digestive tract of some birds used to grind up food and aided with grit or stone particles

Gleaning - a bird strategy used to catch insect prey

Grooming - the act of preening and self-cleaning

Iris - colored outer ring surrounding birds' pupil

Lek - male aggression when in competition for the attention of a female

Mantle - front area of a bird's upper portion found between nape and top back
Migration - seasonal movement of birds

Morph - a polymorphic plumage color variance between the same species

Molt - a periodic shedding and replacement of feathers

Nail - hard tissue at the tip of a bird's beak

Nares - two holes leading to the nasal cavities in the bird's skull

Nest - a bird's lair and home; where a female lays eggs and roosts

Over brooding - a phenomenon when birds continue to brood eggs not likely to hatch

Passerine - any bird of the order Passeriformes

Pinioning - the removal of the joint of a bird's wing farthest from the body preventing flight

Plumage - refers to feathers covering a bird as well as pattern, color and arrangement of feathers

Plumology - the study of feathers

Pre-alternate molt - also known as the prenuptial moult when basic plumage is shed to make way for nuptial plumage

Prebasic molt - moult birds go through after breeding season

Precocial - young birds that after hatched has their eyes open

Preening - grooming od feathers in birds
Quill - the main stem of a feather where all structures branch from

Resident - a non-migratory bird

Rectal bristles stiff, tapering feathers around the eyes of some birds

Rosette - a found at the corners of the beaks of some birds. A fleshy rosette area

Rump - area of a bird's body between the end of the back and the base of the tail

Sexual dimorphism - common occurrence amongst birds in which males and females of a similar sort display different character traits

Song - bird vocalization associated with courtship

Speculum - A patch of typically bright colored feathers, often iridescent

Sternum - bird's breastbone

Syrinx - the vocal organs of birds

Tail streamers - narrow tips of the tail of some birds

Talon - claw of bird of prey

Teleoptiles - feathers of an adult bird

Throat - body area located between the chin and the upper part of the breast

Thigh - body part between knee and trunk of the bird's body

Vent - the outer opening of the cloaca

Wings - The bird's forelimbs that are the essential to flight

Wingspan - distance between wings from one wing tip to the other

Zoonosis - a zoonosis is any disease of animals that can be contracted by a human being

Index

A

accessories 14, 44, 45, 84, 130, 140, 148
animal movement license 52
Aspergillosis 127, 128, 129, 130
Asymptomatic 123, 125, 126
Aviary 56, 57

B

behavior 11, 40, 41, 137
breeder 13, 49, 53, 54, 55, 82, 110, 114, 116
breeding 11, 12, 109, 110, 111, 112, 113, 114, 115, 141, 149
brooding 114

C

cage 140, 43, 44, 45, 47, 84, 85, 86, 87, 88, 89, 92, 99, 130, 137, 140, 146
calcium 100, 101, 141
CITES 50, 51, 52
clutch 11, 54, 111, 113, 114, 142
cost 39, 40, 43, 44, 45, 46, 47, 48
cyanosis 128
cuttlebone 100, 140, 141

D

diagnosis 126, 129, 131, 133, 134, 135
diet 12, 46, 54, 89, 90, 93, 94, 95, 99, 100, 130, 139, 141, 150
diseases 13, 52, 94, 99, 113, 119, 120, 121, 135
dishes 44, 88, 89, 130, 140, 148
DNA 11, 110, 131, 132

droppings 89, 113, 136

E

E-Coli 11, 12, 99, 100, 111, 113, 114, 115, 139, 142
eggs 42, 85, 113, 127, 130
environment 17, 37, 39, 44, 69, 70, 72, 82
eyes 20, 21, 82, 121, 125, 128, 137

F

family 10, 12, 14, 139
feather 9, 10, 40, 42, 82, 91, 99, 131, 136, 137
feeding 44, 46, 93, 94, 95, 130
female 11, 109, 110, 111, 114, 142
food 46, 47, 48, 84, 86, 88, 89, 90, 94, 102, 136, 140, 141, 142, 150
fruits 46, 90, 93, 97, 99, 102, 130, 141

G

genus 16, 17, 18, 25, 26, 27, 28, 29
Great Britain 50, 52, 53, 78, 146, 147
grooming 43, 45, 91, 106, 107, 140

H

habitat 12, 27, 85, 137, 139
handling 91, 103
hatching 114, 142
health 52, 54, 82, 86, 88, 89, 120, 123, 131, 135, 137
history 7, 23, 55
hygiene 45, 91

I

illness 95, 121, 123, 127, 135
immune system 95, 122, 123, 127, 130

incubation 11, 12, 111, 114, 115, 139, 142
infection 120, 121, 122, 123, 124, 125, 128, 129, 132, 133, 134, 135, 137
initial costs 43

L

lay 142
license 52
lifespan 2, 11, 12, 139
longevity 82

M

male 109, 110
mating 111
maturity 11, 12, 110, 111, 114, 139, 142

N

nails 91, 103, 106, 107, 130, 131
nest 111, 113, 114, 115, 140, 142
nesting 113, 114
nutrients 89, 90, 93, 94, 95
nutritional 46, 93, 94, 141
needs 45, 46, 47, 84, 85, 86, 88, 91, 94, 99, 131

O

oil 91, 143
order 12, 85, 94, 112, 139

P

Pacheco's Disease 126
parrots 2, 3, 8, 9, 11, 42, 45, 47, 90, 92, 94, 97, 102
PBFD virus 130
pellet 46, 89, 90, 94, 95, 99, 140

perches 44, 86, 88, 89, 130, 140, 142, 143
permit 49, 51, 52
pet store 13, 45, 46, 53, 54, 89, 107
prevention 119, 130, 132, 137
Psittacosis 125, 126

Q

quick 12, 14, 15, 18, 105

R

reproduction 11, 110, 111, 113
respiratory 91, 121, 122, 125, 127, 128, 129, 133, 137, 143

S

seeds 11, 12, 46, 89, 90, 93, 94, 96, 97, 103, 130, 139, 141, 143, 150
seed mix 89, 140, 141
sexing 11, 110, 141
sexually dimorphic 11, 12, 110, 139, 141
species 9, 13, 106, 115, 120, 124, 127, 129, 130, 142
symptoms 119, 120, 121, 122, 123, 124, 125, 126, 127, 131, 133, 134

T

taming 104
training 102, 103, 105, 106, 143
temperature 91, 92, 111, 140
toys 35, 43, 44, 45, 47, 89, 140, 142, 148
Treats 46, 90, 102
treatment 47, 101, 120, 121, 122, 124, 129, 130, 132, 134
types 9, 14, 18, 35, 36, 37, 39, 41, 42, 47, 88, 90, 94, 141

U

United States 13, 26, 27, 50, 51, 52, 55, 116, 146

V

vegetables 46, 90, 95, 99, 130, 141, 127
ventilation 127
veterinarian 91, 97, 99, 107, 108, 135, 137, 143
virus. 120, 121, 122, 123, 124, 126, 127, 131, 132

W

water 86, 87, 88, 89, 90, 91, 101
wild 37, 42, 50, 88, 93, 94, 106, 113
wingspan 11, 12, 19, 20, 21, 25, 28, 31, 32

Photo Credits

Page 1 Photo by user Wow_Pho via Pixabay.com, https://pixabay.com/en/animal-australia-background-beak-1226216/

Page 5 Photo by user Skitterphoto via Pixabay.com, https://pixabay.com/en/parrot-colorful-bird-feathers-lory-777218/

Page 28 Photo by user Wow_Pho via Pixabay.com, https://pixabay.com/en/animal-aviary-background-beak-bird-1153410/

Page 37 Photo by user Magnaduf via Pixabay.com, https://pixabay.com/en/birds-lori-animal-lori-red-beak-1005961/

Page 49 Photo by user Hans via Pixabay.com, https://pixabay.com/en/lori-parrot-drink-eat-feeding-406640/

Page 76 Photo by user endachs via Pixabay.com, https://pixabay.com/en/parakeet-bird-lorikeet-parrot-lori-292797/

Page 85 Photo by user ddouk via Pixabay.com,

https://pixabay.com/en/rainbow-lorikeet-lori-red-638411/

Page 93 Photo by user Wow_Pho via Pixabay.com, https://pixabay.com/en/animal-australia-background-beak-1223868/

Page 100 Photo by user BM10777 via Pixabay.com, https://pixabay.com/en/lorikeet-bird-wedge-tail-lori-185775/

References

"Common Diseases of Lories & Lorikeets and Health Program" – BeautyofBirds.com
https://www.beautyofbirds.com/lorikeethealthprogram.html

"Hybrids and Mutations" – Lory Link
http://www.kcbbs.gen.nz/lori/ar/mutation.html

"Lories and Lorikeets" – Wikipedia.org
https://en.wikipedia.org/wiki/Lories_and_lorikeets

"Lories in Captivity – as Pets, Aviary Birds or Breeders" – BeautyofBirds.com
https://www.beautyofbirds.com/loriesaspets.html

"Lories & Lorikeet" – AquaticCommunity.com
http://www.aquaticcommunity.com/lories/

"Lories & Lorikeet" – Petyak.com
http://www.petyak.com/birds/general-bird/articles/lories-lorikeets/

"Lorikeet Genetics 101" – LisaLories.com
http://lisaslories.com/lorikeet-genetics-101/

"Lory and Lorikeet" – Petco.com

https://www.petco.com/content/petco/PetcoStore/en_US/pet-services/resource-center/caresheets/lory-and-lorikeet.html

"Lory and Lorikeet" – San Diego Zoo
http://animals.sandiegozoo.org/animals/lory-and-lorikeet

"Mixing Different Species of Bird" – Birdsville.net
http://birdsville.net.au/pet-bird-advice-and-training/mixing-different-species-of-bird/

"Not All Birds are Endangered" – The Parrot Society UK
http://www.theparrotsocietyuk.org/conservation/conservation-articles/not-all-birds-are-endangered

"Supporting Parrots in Rescues and Parrot Sanctuaries" – Good Bird Inc.
http://www.goodbirdinc.com/parrotsanctuaries.html

Feeding Baby
Cynthia Cherry
978-1941070000

Axolotl
Lolly Brown
978-0989658430

Dysautonomia, POTS Syndrome
Frederick Earlstein
978-0989658485

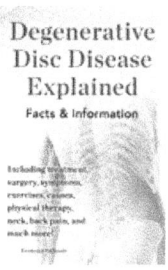

Degenerative Disc Disease Explained
Frederick Earlstein
978-0989658485

Sinusitis, Hay Fever,
Allergic Rhinitis Explained
Frederick Earlstein
978-1941070024

Wicca
Riley Star
978-1941070130

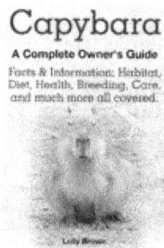

Zombie Apocalypse
Rex Cutty
978-1941070154

Capybara
Lolly Brown
978-1941070062

Eels As Pets
Lolly Brown
978-1941070167

Scabies and Lice Explained
Frederick Earlstein
978-1941070017

Saltwater Fish As Pets
Lolly Brown
978-0989658461

Torticollis Explained
Frederick Earlstein
978-1941070055

Kennel Cough
Lolly Brown
978-0989658409

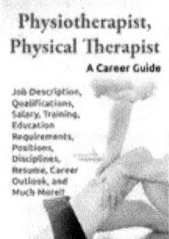

Physiotherapist, Physical Therapist
Christopher Wright
978-0989658492

Rats, Mice, and Dormice As Pets
Lolly Brown
978-1941070079

Wallaby and Wallaroo Care
Lolly Brown
978-1941070031

Bodybuilding Supplements
Explained
Jon Shelton
978-1941070239

Demonology
Riley Star
978-19401070314

Pigeon Racing
Lolly Brown
978-1941070307

Dwarf Hamster
Lolly Brown
978-1941070390

Cryptozoology
Rex Cutty
978-1941070406

Eye Strain
Frederick Earlstein
978-1941070369

Inez The Miniature Elephant
Asher Ray
978-1941070353

Vampire Apocalypse
Rex Cutty
978-1941070321

www.ingramcontent.com/pod-product-compliance
Lightning Source LLC
LaVergne TN
LVHW051644080426
835511LV00016B/2491